HOW TO GRO'

Your Gard

CW01457154

David Oconner

©Copyright 2012 David Oconner

ISBN-13:978-1475079623

All rights reserved. No part of this publication may be reproduced or distributed in any form or by any means, electronic or mechanical, or stored in a database or retrieval system, without prior written permission from the publisher.

Introduction

A vegetable garden at home is the easiest way to ensure a great supply of juicy tomatoes all year round! You will not have to rely on the less-than-fresh produce available in supermarkets that are most likely filled with chemicals. Growing tomatoes at home means you can not only prepare a fresh salad everyday, but also enjoy hours of fun in the garden.

Tomatoes are one of the easiest plants to grow and with a little care you can savor a new tomato recipe everyday. Whether you like them freshly chopped, sun dried, pickled or in sauces, tomatoes are a great source of nutrients that make your food tasty and fill it with nutritional goodness.

Tomatoes are rich in vitamins and essential micronutrients. These juicy fruits contain micronutrients like folates and vitamins A, C, E, and K. Tomatoes are also rich in electrolytes like sodium and potassium as well as minerals like iron, manganese, calcium, zinc, phosphorus and magnesium. Thanks to the beta-carotene present in tomatoes, they offer a myriad of health benefits.

Tomatoes are extremely low-fat and low-calorie, making them the perfect snack for your healthy everyday diet. The rich reserves of vitamins found in tomatoes make them an effective anti-oxidant that cleans the blood stream, improves eyesight, strengthens bones, and prevents cell damage.

The large reserves of potassium and vitamin B keep blood pressure and cholesterol levels in control, making tomatoes useful in battling heart troubles, diabetes and cancer. Tomatoes are excellent supplements to maintain strong, glowing and naturally resilient hair, skin and teeth.

Different Varieties of Tomatoes

After you have decided to grow a tomato garden at home, there are several details you must tend to. Tomato plants are available in several varieties and picking the right one can make a world of difference. Take out some time to differentiate between unique varieties of tomato plants that can best suit the gardening options available to you.

Determinate

Determinate varieties of tomato plants grow and bear fruit for a specific period in the season and stop producing fruit thereafter. Some of the most popular varieties of determinate tomato plants include Northern Exposure, Celebrity, Marglobe, Doublerich, Floramerica, Heatwave, New Yorker, Solar Fire, Oregon Spring, and Rutgers.

Determinate varieties of tomato plants mature earlier than indeterminate plants, produce fewer fruits and are generally shorter. This variety stops growing once the fruits are borne and do not produce for a long time.

Indeterminate

Unlike determinate varieties, indeterminate tomato plants continue growing throughout the season and produce larger amounts of fruit at a time that take longer to mature. Shoots and side branches of indeterminate tomato plants continue growing even after new fruits have begun to grow. These plants continue to bear fruit until they are stopped by natural forces like frost, diseases or pest infestation or cut down manually.

Some of the popular indeterminate tomato varieties include Brandywine, Better Boy, Big Beef, Juliet, Early Girl, Jetstar, Delicious, and Mortgage Lifter. Indeterminate plans are preferred over determinate varieties as they offer larger yield and help gardeners detect problems with the soil, water and fertilizer in the early stages of plantation.

Dwarf

Dwarf determinate tomato varieties are usually shorter and stronger than regular determinate tomato plants. Growing a few feet in height, dwarf tomato plants can be planted in pots and smaller containers. Producing all their fruit at once, dwarf varieties stop bearing fruit for the rest of the season. Cherry tomatoes are one of the most popular dwarf varieties and make for excellent patio plants.

Patio, Tiny Tim, Red Robin, Cherry Gold, Small Fry, Yellow Canary and Pixie Hybrid are some of the most popular varieties of dwarf tomato plants suitable for containers.

Dwarf indeterminate

Possibly the most favored of tomato plant varieties, indeterminate dwarf plants are small in size but provide a great crop yield. Although they do not grow taller than three or four feet in height, indeterminate dwarf plants produce large juicy tomatoes throughout the season. These plants can be grown equally well in spacious gardens and smaller containers. As long as the ideal natural environment is maintained, these plants can continue producing tomatoes unless spoilt by infection, disease or frost.

Bush Big Boy, and Husky Hybrids in red, pink and gold are popular picks for indeterminate dwarf tomato varieties.

Other ways to categorize tomato plants

Tomato plants can be categorized in other ways to help you find the most suitable variety for your garden.

Heirloom v Hybrid

Also known as open pollinated tomatoes, heirloom tomato varieties produce pure seeds year after year. These seeds can be saved for years and when planted, replicate the same variety. Particularly praised for their distinct flavor and taste, heirloom tomato plants are available in many colors.

It is believed that a tomato variety is required to be at least fifty years old before it achieves the heirloom status. Some of the most popular heirloom tomato varieties include Brandywine, Stupice, Cherokee Purple, Green Grape and Mortgage Lifter.

Hybrid tomatoes are produced by seeds cross pollinated with other varieties and always produce unique results. Recently developed hybrids are known for their outstanding flavors and unique textures.

Unlike heirloom tomatoes, seeds found in hybrid tomatoes will neither produce exact results nor retain all of the original traits of the parent. Hybrid tomato varieties are built for disease resistance and high production. Early Girl, Sun Gold and Sweet 100 are popular hybrid tomato varieties.

Appearance (color, shape, size)

Tomato plants can also be chosen based on the appearance of the fruit they will bear. While the traditional tomato is a round red fruit, several variations have cropped up over the years. Apart from the regular red, you can opt to produce yellow, green, orange, pink, white, black and striped tomatoes.

Popular varieties of colored tomato plants include Pink Girl, Mountain Gold, Lemon Boy, White Wonder, Evergreen, and Long Keeper. These varieties of tomato plants are generally indeterminate and are known to produce large amounts of juicy tomatoes.

Tomatoes can also be produced in shapes other than round and newer varieties are being developed everyday. Interesting shape variations of the regular round fruit include grape, cherry, egg, pear, flattened and oblong. Plant varieties that produce interestingly shaped tomatoes include Banana Legs, Anna Russian, Black Plum, Giraffe, Jaffa, and Watermelon Beefsteak.

Purpose

The tomato plant variety most suitable for you depends on how you intend to use the produce. If you are planning to use raw tomatoes for salads, main crop tomatoes like cherry tomatoes are perfect for you. Large beefsteak varieties of tomato are large, juicy and ideal for placing in burgers.

Choose paste tomato varieties if you are planning to use them in Italian sauces or store them in cans. As paste tomato plants produce fruits with few seeds and a meaty center, they are preferred for canning. These pear shaped tomatoes are usually without a core. San Marzano, Roma, and Viva Italia are considered the best choices to dish up a delicious sauce.

Choosing the Right Variety

Not every variety of tomato can be grown in your backyard as tomato plants require specific natural conditions and culture practices. Right from your garden size to the purpose of cultivation will make a difference when zeroing in on a suitable tomato variety. As no particular variety of tomato promises the best performance in all parts of the world, it is important to consider the seasonal effects your region will have on the plant.

Ideal environmental conditions

Most needs for tomato plants remain the same with a few exceptions depending on the variety. The preferred climate setting for any tomato variety is similar. Tomato plants grow excellently in warm and sunny regions. Temperatures between 70° F to 80° F (21° C to 27° C) are optimum and promote healthy growth for all varieties of tomato plants.

The soil also plays an important role in cultivating a healthy crop. Moist (not waterlogged) soil with an almost neutral pH of 6 - 6.7 are ideal for tomato plants. Well drained loam soil with medium to rich fertility levels aid healthy growth in tomatoes.

Culture

Tomato plants are tender annual plants i.e. they cannot survive in the cold months and stop producing as soon as the first frost hits. Temperatures colder than 55° F (13° C) are not suitable for tomato plants. It is advisable to plant seeds only when the soil is sufficiently warm and the minimum night time temperatures are well above freezing.

If you are planning to plant seeds indoors, you can start about five to seven weeks before the winter recedes. Transplant the saplings only after the frost has completely retreated. While transplanting or planting seeds outdoors, maintain a space of eighteen to thirty six inches between plants and rows and about thirty six inches in depth.

Common culture practices

Tomato plants are popular among amateur and experienced gardeners as they yield large crops with limited space and are low on maintenance. If tended to carefully, each regular sized tomato plant can produce between ten and fifteen pounds of tomatoes each season. While most tomato plants are cultivated in warmer summer months, some varieties are known to grow well even in low temperatures around spring.

Tomato plants are generally planted indoors weeks in advance and then transplanted. If you are not supplemented by a south facing window that provides adequate sunlight, you may have to arrange for additional light sources. Alternatively, you can also opt for saplings or plant seeds outdoors directly. If you are planning to purchase saplings, ensure that the transplants are 6 to 10 inches in height and appear stocky and healthy.

Disease resistance

To ensure high production yield, it is important to choose tomato plant varieties with strong resistance against common diseases. Plants vulnerable to diseases weaken the crop and prevent it from providing a healthy yield. Some of the most common plant diseases that affect tomato crops include verticillium, fusarium, tobacco mosaic, root knot nematode, and alternaria.

Most tomato varieties are resistant to common soil borne diseases and are labeled accordingly on the seed packet. Tomato varieties marked F or V are resistant to verticillium and fusarium. If crops in your region are susceptible to other diseases, look for diseases resistance markings like A for Alternaria, T for Tobacco Mosaic virus and N for root knot nematode. Ensure that you conduct enough research about the specific planting conditions in your region and purchase tomato varieties accordingly.

Maturity time

Tomato plants take anywhere between 55 days and 105 days to mature. The time a tomato plant takes to fully mature depends on the variety and the local climate. If you live in a colder region where winter dominates most of the year, it is better to opt for tomato plants varieties that bear fruit in shorter periods.

Most tomato crops like beefsteak varieties require ninety days to fully mature while other plants bear fruit in about ten weeks. If you are looking for tomato varieties that ripen comparatively quickly, you can opt for Sun Gold cherry tomatoes that bear fruit in about 65 days or Juliet that yield large production in sixty days.

Growth habits

The growth habits of different tomato varieties make a big difference in achieving optimum crop yield. Choosing a tomato variety based on its growth habit and providing the necessary equipment to ensure maximum yield are two essential steps you must take. If you are planning on enjoying a full crop, adequate space, support and nutrients should be supplied.

In terms of growth habits, tomato plants are mainly divided into determinate and indeterminate varieties. If you have limited space in your backyard or are planting tomato seeds in a pot, determinate plants are the answer. This variety grows to a fixed height of two to three feet and bears fruit in specific months of the season only. Determinate tomato plants are also useful for gardeners living in colder regions as ripe fruits arrive much faster than indeterminate varieties. Paste tomatoes and dwarf varieties are generally determinate.

If you are blessed with a large space to plant tomatoes, you should opt for indeterminate plants. Indeterminate varieties are mainly consist of vines and can grow several feet. This variety provides great tomatoes all through the season until the frost sets. Indeterminate plants are also beneficial to those living in warmer regions as they can enjoy a larger crop. You should provide stakes, ladders and cages for indeterminate varieties as they tend to spread out. With proper support, these plants can yield substantial crops.

You can also opt for semi-determinate tomato varieties that are a mix of determinate and indeterminate plants. Growing upto heights of four to six feet, these plants take longer than determinate tomato varieties to produce mature fruit.

Winter storage

If you are living in colder regions, you can also choose to harvest fruits before they are fully ripe. Winter storage tomato varieties are planted later than regular tomatoes and harvested when they partially ripe. This method helps preserve tomatoes for longer as the frost sets in. If stored in the right conditions, these tomatoes can stay fresh for three months or longer.

Different Ways to Grow Tomatoes

Although there are several specifications you must tend to when it comes to soil quality, fertilizers and seedlings, tomato plants can be grown in a number of ways. While most prefer to grow tomatoes outdoors, not everyone lives in regions naturally suited for tomatoes. As they require slightly warmer climates, gardeners in colder regions seek other methods to cultivate tomatoes at home.

Container gardening

If you are interesting in growing tomatoes at home but do not have a spacious backyard, you can grow these juicy delights in smaller containers. Container gardening offers the added convenience of conserving space and allows you to cultivate tomatoes indoors or outdoors.

As tomato plants grow an average of six to seven feet in height, it is important to choose larger containers. Make sure that you use containers of at least 14 inches in diameter as smaller containers do not provide adequate space and nutrients and tomato plants may not survive the season. The crop yield in small containers is also limited.

Instead of regular garden soil, opt for rich potting soil as it helps prevent compaction. Evaluate the soil composition and add the necessary nutrients to ensure full growth of the tomato plants. If the large containers have holes on the bottom, cover them with small stones to prevent losing soil every time you water the plants. Staking is another measure you can take to ensure that the branches remain in place. This also allows you to protect the tomato plants against parasites and other pests.

Bale gardening

An innovative method to grow tomatoes is in hay bales. Bale gardening is a relatively newer method that is grabbing the attention of creative home gardeners. Although it may seem unlikely, tomato plants grow excellently in bales of hay. If you live in a spacious and pleasantly sunny region, bale gardening could be perfect for you.

As hay is also susceptible to weeds, wheat straw and oat straws are recommended. Bind together long pieces of straw with wires and synthetic binding material to keep the bale intact. It is believed that bales bound horizontally and straws aligned vertically are particularly helpful in creating strong root systems in tomato plants. Since hay is naturally porous, these bales act as natural hydroponic systems.

It is important to continue watering the bales as dry hay could damage tomato plants severely. At least ten days before planting, ensure that you water the hay bales twice a day and add nitrogen rich fertilizers every alternate day. After adding the fertilizer, continue watering the bales for four more days. You can then add generous amounts of soil and compost on top of the bales before planting. It is best that you use not more than 2 tomato plants for each bale. When the growing season has retreated, you can break up the bale and use the straw for mulch. Start with a fresh bale of straw every season.

Greenhouse cultivation

Greenhouse cultivation of tomato plants is most suitable in regions that cannot naturally fulfill the ideal requirements. The cultivation process of tomato plants in greenhouses is slightly different compared to outdoor cultivation but produces the same results.

If you are using a greenhouse to grow tomatoes at home, you should start by sowing seeds between January and March when the temperatures are between 60° F to 65° F (16° C to 18° C). The seedlings are then planted two inches apart in boxes filled with potting compost. They are then moved to 3-inch pots with similar compost and planted individually when small leaves appear.

As the plant grows bigger, they are transplanted into nine inch pots in a mixture of loamy soil and potting compost. Alternatively, you can also use large soil beds with the same composition and space the tomato plants about 18 inches apart, leaving three feet between rows.

Each tomato plant is restricted to a single main stem and all side shoots are removed as soon as they appear. You can tie a cane or a string to the main stem for extra support. Fertilizer must be added to the plants once a week after the first fruits appear. Young tomato plants should be watered moderately initially with increasing amounts as it grows. The optimum temperature for greenhouse cultivation of tomato plants is between 55° F and 75° F (13° C to 24° C).

Ring culture

Growing tomato plants with ring cultures has become popular as it promises a great yield with less soil and fewer risks of infection. Ring culture mainly works on the principle where feeding roots are supplied with a limited amount of suitable compost with a regular supply of water. A sterile material (peat, sand or ashes) is used to create a moist bed that supplies water to the lower roots.

If you are growing tomatoes with ring culture, it is important to keep the bed moist at all times to prevent the plant from drying. Plants are placed in bottomless ring shaped pots and filled with potting compost. You should supply generous amounts of water for the few weeks of plantation and add fertilizers on a weekly basis.

Hydroponics

Hydroponics is cultivation method that is quickly catching on and you can avoid paying exorbitant amounts by growing tomatoes through hydroponics at home. However, hydroponics requires many specific needs to generate a great yield. From light sources, temperatures, humidity levels and fertilizers, there are many details you should keep in mind.

Growing tomato plants can be slightly tricky as the right amount of sunshine can produce amazing results while little or extra sunshine can ruin the same. Theoretically, tomato plants require eighteen hours of sunlight in a day. As they mostly absorb the blue part of the spectrum, a high intensity metal halide discharge lamp works best indoors. Studies have proved that this type of lighting can increase productivity upto 30%. However, if you have access to adequate sunshine, you need not invest in artificial lighting.

Ideally, tomato plants require day time temperatures of 70° F to 80° F (22° C to 26° C) and night time temperatures of 10° F (5° C). In terms of humidity, hydroponic tomatoes require a day time humidity of 70% and about 80% at night.

Preparing the Soil Bed before Planting Tomatoes

If you want to ensure a great yield from your tomato plants, it is important to prepare the soil well. Creating the ideal soil conditions includes several small steps that make a big difference by the end of the season. Follow these simple steps to make your garden soil perfect and enjoy large quantities of juicy tomatoes in the seasons to come.

Tilling

Tilling is an important step to keep the soil aerated and healthy. Over the years, gardeners have realized the benefits of soil-dwelling organisms like earthworms and other microorganisms, and the practice of tilling has become less popular. However, certain soils require extensive tilling to preserve their natural nutrition.

Tilling the soil weeks before planting seeds allows you to assess the composition of the soil and add the necessary nutrients most suitable for tomato plants. It is essential to till soil if the plot has been used consistently for different crops. As used plots are generally low on fresh organic matter and nutrients, it is essential to rejuvenate the soil and allow a richer tomato crop to grow.

Soil with large amounts of clay or sand should be tilled extensively. Soil rich in clay is generally much heavier and holds excessive water. This property is not suitable for tomato plants as excessive moisture could cause diseases and improper growth. On the other hand, sandy soil cannot retain water for long and is generally low on nutrients. Both soil types require unique nutrients to create a composition rich in nutrients.

Warming the soil

Tomato plants grow much better in warmer soils. Soil takes longer than air to adjust to warmer temperatures. If the soil has not caught up with the increasing temperatures, you can cover the tomato plot with black plastic to accelerate the heating process. These plastic sheets are easily available in nurseries and home improvement stores.

You can start the warming process a few weeks before planting the seedlings. Secure the black plastic over the selected plot with bricks, rocks and other heavy items. While planting the seeds, you can choose to remove it completely or use it to deter weeds from growing around the new tomato plants.

Soil composition: pH levels

One of the most important properties of the soil that you should check is the pH level. A single pH test is enough for a small patch for land. However, if you are planting multiple rows of tomatoes, you should carry out pH tests in different parts of the plot.

If you are new to testing pH levels in soil, it is helpful to read up on what the different levels indicate. pH is measured from a scale of 0 to 14 where 0 stands for highly acidic, 14 stands for highly alkaline and 7 is considered neutral. Tomatoes are known to grow best in mildly acidic soils between the pH levels of 6.5 and 7.0.

Acidic soil

Acidic soils with pH lower than 6 are considered unsuitable to grow tomatoes. You can counter this acidity by adding alkaline substances in the soil. Lime does an excellent job of lowering the soil's acidity and brings it to the optimum range. For best results, incorporate lime into the soil at least six months before planting.

Alkaline soil

pH levels higher than 7 indicate alkaline soils that contain insufficient organic matter. This can be countered by adding acidic products to reduce the alkalinity. Substances like elemental sulfur provide the much needed nutrient boost and balance the pH of the soil most suitable for tomato plants. You can also add peat moss to introduce more organic matter into alkaline soil.

Evaluating nutrients

Essential soil nutrients that aid growth of healthy tomato plants include nitrogen, potassium and phosphorus. By evaluating the nutrients in your soil, you can correct deficiencies and create the ideal soil composition for tomato plants.

Nitrogen

Nitrogen is essential to keep the tomato plants healthy and the leaves green. If your tomato plants are displaying slow growth or yellowing leaves, this indicates nitrogen deficiency. However, introducing the right amount of nitrogen is essential as excess of the nutrient can cause the stems to become large and leaves soft. The flower production also decreases with excessive nitrogen. Ideally, tomato plants require 1.75 pounds of nitrogen every 500 sqft that should be incorporated shortly before planting.

Organic fertilizers that are good sources of nitrogen include compost, alfalfa meal, fish meal, legumes and feather meal. Inorganic nitrogen-rich fertilizers include ammonium nitrate, potassium nitrate, urea and sodium nitrate.

Potassium

Disease resistance and growth are also supported by potassium. Unlike phosphorus and nitrogen, potassium should be incorporated into the soil in the winter. Slow growth, weak plants and leaves with brown edges are a common indication of potassium deficiency and can be fixed with potassium rich fertilizers.

Popular organic fertilizers that provide potassium to tomato plants include granite dust and wood ash while inorganic fertilizers like rock sand and potassium sulfate are also used commonly.

Phosphorus

Phosphorus plays an important role in developing strong roots for tomato plants. It also helps the formation of seeds, cultivation of fruits and builds resistance against common plant diseases. Phosphorus deficiency can cause reddened stem and leaves and stunt the growth of tomato plants. Fertilizers rich in phosphorus should be introduced into the soil before planting instead of sprinkling on the surface.

Organic fertilizers rich in phosphorus include compost and bone meal while inorganic fertilizers are rock phosphate and super phosphate.

Importance of compost for nutrient rich soil

Compost itself is not rich in nutrients but plays an important role in improving the quality of soil. Comprising naturally broken down organic matter, compost greatly improves the structure and cultivability of the soil. It also improves the soil's ability to retain nutrients, and attracts earthworms and microbes. Compost protects plants from common diseases and reduces compaction. It is a good idea to add compost to any type of soil before planting your tomatoes.

Planting Tomatoes at Home

Tomato seeds are generally planted indoors and nurtured until they reach a certain stage. When the seedlings are approximately six inches in height, they are ready to be planted outdoors. It is best if you transplant tomatoes and plant them outdoors on cloudy days as the saplings are protected from sudden dry outs or surge in temperatures.

To begin transplanting, start by pinching off lower leaves in the tomato plant. If you have grown the seedling yourself, this process will be familiar to you.

Lightly bathe the tomato seedlings with weak compost tea before you transplant them. Avoid using strong fertilizers as the tender seedlings could undergo a 'shock'.

Add one cup each of kelp meal and bone meal into every planting hole before you transplant the tomato seedlings. This instantly improves the soil quality, fertility and nutrition. Both slow release fertilizers are rich in micronutrients with kelp meal providing all around nutrients and bone meal boosting the growth of flowers and fruits with its phosphorus-rich composition.

You can also add 1-2 tablespoons of Epson salt in each planting hole and provide your tomato seedlings with added magnesium.

Ensure that you handle the plants carefully as any damage or bruising may leave them vulnerable to plant diseases, infections and pests. Keep the leaves clear of dirt to prevent viruses and fungi living in the soil from infecting the plant.

If you are living in colder regions, plant both the roots and a large section of the stem in the hole to accommodate a larger root system. This helps the tomato plant develop a strong and stable base to absorb more nutrients.

If the tomato seedlings have developed tall and leggy stems, you can support them with trench planting. Trench planting has two main advantages; it will save you the trouble of digging deep holes and the shallow planting of the seedling will ensure maximum absorption of nutrients and warmth. To incorporate trench planting into your tomato plantation:

Start by digging a horizontal trench long enough to accommodate all the plants.

Except for the top leaf branch, remove all other leaves from the plant.

Lay the tomato plant inside the trench on its side to cover the root and bare stem with the recommended soil mixture of kelp meal and bone meal. Put a layer of soil of 2-3 inches thickness over the trench.

After you have filled the trench with soil, you may notice that the rest of the plant is still lying on the dirt. You need not worry about it as the plant will soon grow vertically with the aid of sunlight.

You can place a rock under the plant to elevate it and push it to the right direction. If the next few days are bound to be rainy or cloudy, it is better to place the rock.

In warmer regions with longer summers, it is better not to bury the stem as the plant is more vulnerable to fungus. The long summer months offer more time for the plant to develop its root structure and retain nutrients without the need for deep soil planting.

Trellising

Trellising tomatoes is an important step you should take especially if you have limited space in your backyard. Trellising is a fairly simple process and offers many advantages.

By trellising tomatoes, you can grow more varieties and a greater number in a smaller space. As trellised tomatoes have smaller root structures, you can accommodate more plants without compromising on quality and care. Trellising tomato plants allows you to channel all the plant's energy into its fruit. This results in larger, tastier and juicier tomatoes that almost always mature earlier than regular plants.

Trellising also helps you maintain a neat garden and challenges your gardening skills. And as always, a neat looking garden is a matter of pride in your neighborhood. The initial trellising process takes about half hour along with a short weekly session to train the tomato plants. Trellising is more beneficial to indeterminate tomato varieties as they produce large yields for longer.

You can start trellising your tomato garden by purchasing 4x4 cedar posts (8 feet long), strong nylon strings, stainless steel pipes or tension wires (8-14 feet) and twine.

Use the cedar posts to set up a frame for the strings. Digs holes about 2-3 feet deep to accommodate the posts at each end of the planting rows.

Drill holes towards the top of the posts with a diameter large enough for the steel pipe. Place the pipe in the holes and ensure that the structure is standing erect and stable. Your trellising frame is ready.

Place the tomato plants with a gap of 24 inches in a straight line or in a zigzag fashion.

Transplant the tomato plants from the pots and into the ground. If you are planting tall seedlings, provide support.

Suspend nylon string or wire over each tomato plant and ensure that it can carry weights upto 25 pounds. Weaker nylon strings may not be able to carry growing tomato plants and end up damaging the vines. Wait for the tomato plants to grow at least 1-2 feet in height before you wrap the nylon string around the main stem.

If you are planning to support the tomato seedlings with stakes, it is better to place them at the time of transplant as driving stakes through developed plants could damage the roots. Place the stakes downwind of the plants so that they provide adequate support on windy days.

After you have completed trellising your tomato garden, you can move on pruning the tomatoes.

Pruning

If you are planning to grow tomatoes in your backyard, your focus should be on producing maximum yield with great flavors. This can be achieved if you prune the tomato plants properly and ensure that all the nutrients are reaching the fruit. One way to channel the nutrients to the fruit is to cut off additional growing tips and stick to a single stem.

Removing unwanted suckers

It is a good idea to get rid of growing suckers in the early stages as smaller wounds heal quickly. If you wait too long to remove unwanted shoots, it may damage the plant and lead to infection. To remove young shoots, grab the sucker with your thumb and index finger and gently bend it back and forth till it snaps. This process is known as simple pruning.

You can also pinch out the tip of the shoot and leave behind a few leaves to protect developing fruits and for photosynthesis. Allow a few fruit bearing shoots to grow from a single stem and remove additional shoots to leave the central stem intact.

Removing leaves

Removing older leaves in maturing tomato plants is an essential step to speed up the fruiting process. As the tomato plants mature, the lower leaves will turn yellow and wilt. This is a natural process that is observed in all healthy tomato plants.

If you find yellowing leaves on your tomato plants, remove them immediately to make better use of the nutrients and prevent diseases from spreading to the fruit. Removing yellowed leaves gives the plant a greener and healthier look and protects the fruit from infection and malnutrition.

Topping the plant

This step is carried out about a month before the first frost hits. Remove the terminal shoot of the tomato plant to give the fruits limited time to mature. This directs all the nutrients to the fruit and results in juicier, tastier and healthier tomatoes.

Like trellising, pruning is not required for determinate tomato varieties as they exhibit limited growth.

Although you can use blades and other cutting tools to remove shoots, it is better to use your own hands. Using improperly sterilized equipment could lead to infection. While it is easier to use hands for tender shoots, older ones may require blades.

Wash your hands thoroughly before handling tomato plants, especially if you are a smoker. Tomato plants are susceptible to tobacco mosaic virus that is commonly transmitted through tobacco products.

It is important to add adequate fertilizers during the growing season to get the best of pruning tomato plants.

Fertilizing

Tomato plants require the right balance of nutrients to produce a healthy yield of large and juicy tomatoes. Fertilizing the tomatoes is an important way to supply these nutrients through the soil. Some of the most important nutrients that help produce a great batch of tomatoes season after season include nitrogen, potassium, phosphorus, sulfur, and magnesium.

First plantation

Fertilizers should be applied in different stages of plant growth. The first round of fertilizers should be supplied while planting your tomato seedlings. Dig a planting hole about three inches deeper and two inches wider than the plant root. Add three to four tablespoons of fertilizer into the planting hole and set your tomato seedling. Regularly water the young plant to increase absorption of the nutrients present in the fertilizer.

Maturing tomato plants

You should apply a second round of fertilizer when the first tomatoes have appeared. If the tomatoes are small and raw, it is the perfect time to add more fertilizer.

Incorporate dry manure with bone meal to lend balance to the nutrient composition. This combination is preferred among experienced tomato growers with a penchant for tasty and organic tomatoes.

Sprinkle fertilizer mix around the plant, encircling the base. Cover this dry mix with a layer of top soil, two inches thick. Use grass or hay cuttings to coat the soil over the fertilizer and soak the area.

By moistening the soil, you are allowing the tomato plant to absorb the nutrients in the fertilizer. A layer of grass or hay keeps the moisture content in the soil leveled.

Depending on the individual composition of the fertilizer, repeat this process every week or more.

It is important that you prevent direct contact between the tomato plant and the fertilizer. As tomato seedlings are generally sensitive, the strong concentration of the fertilizer may burn the plant and stunt the growth.

You can also spray fertilizer on your tomato plantation to increase the absorption rate of the nutrients. Plants are known to absorb nutrients quicker through leaves in comparison to roots. However, the effects of this process are not as long lasting compared to mixing fertilizer in soil.

Use seaweed mix or fish emulsion and dissolve them in the fertilizer along with water. Spray this combination of fertilizers on the tomato plant every three weeks to protect the plant from malnutrition and common diseases.

With a simple soil test, you can figure out the deficiencies in your soil and introduce the necessary fertilizers.

Organic fertilizers

Most of the recommended fertilizers for tomatoes are composed of an equal ratio of nitrogen, potassium and phosphorus. As much as possible, avoid fertilizers with more nitrogen as they improve leaf and plant growth but limit fruits. In addition to carefully composed fertilizers, tomato plants require soil with abundant organic matter.

Composition of organic fertilizers and necessary supplements

Unlike conventional fertilizers, natural organic compounds are not optimized in terms of the ratio of potassium, phosphorus and nitrogen. Due to the lack of a definite composition, organic fertilizers should be applied carefully. Calculate the unique nutrient needs of your soil and supplement your organic fertilizer.

Some of the most popular supplements include fish emulsion and seaweed.

If you are using organic fertilizers like manure, you should add bone meal to compensate for the natural deficiency in phosphorus. Organic compounds should be applied less frequently than conventional fertilizers as they take longer to break down.

Harvesting Your Tomato Plantation

Harvesting the fruits off your plantation is the most rewarding experience of growing tomatoes at home. When picked in their prime, few delicacies match up to fresh and juicy tomatoes. It is important to pick tomatoes when they are fully ripe and not earlier.

Once you pick a tomato, you are cutting off its oxygen source. However, tomatoes continue ripening even after they are picked off owing to the rich sugar content in the fruit. The processed sugar without a fresh supply of oxygen simply turns into decay promoting compounds like alcohols, ketones and aldehydes. This decay of the processed sugar content in tomatoes affect their taste that does not match upto the fresh taste of perfectly picked tomatoes.

When is the right time?

Depending on the variety of the tomato plant, you can approximate the maturity time and the harvest date. On an average, main crop tomato varieties mature between sixty to eighty-five days after outdoor planting. Determinate and indeterminate varieties of tomato plants have different harvest methods.

Determinate tomato varieties produce a single set of tomatoes within the season. All fruits generally ripen at the same time and can be picked off within two weeks. Determinate tomato plants produce large harvests that are perfect for long term storage. You can freeze the harvested tomatoes or use them to make homemade sauce and tomato juice.

Indeterminate tomato varieties on the other hand, continue producing ripe tomatoes throughout the season. By following a few pruning techniques, you can help your tomato plants produce mature fruits faster. Tomatoes depend on warmth to ripen and not light and will continue to ripen if the weather is cloudy and warm.

How to pick a ripe tomato

If a tomato looks ripe on the outside, it is also ripe on the inside. An easy way to tell a ripe tomato from an immature one is color. If you have opted for a traditional red variety, the tomato will be evenly colored on all sides. The same rule applies to yellow, pink or black tomatoes.

If a tomato is colored red on one side and green on another, it indicates that the fruit is not fully ripe and is unsuitable for harvest. Ripe tomatoes are soft but very firm. If you find the tomatoes on your plants easily squeezable, you may have waited too long.

There are some varieties of tomatoes that should be picked off before they fully ripen. Heirloom tomato varieties tend to become fully ripe before they show color. It is best to harvest heirloom tomatoes when they appear to be almost ripe. Cherry tomatoes develop cracks when left unpicked for too long. They should also be picked off just before they appear fully matured.

To remove tomatoes from the vine, grasp the fruit gently but firmly and continue twisting until they snap off. Alternatively, you can also use small clippers or knives to cut parts of the stem.

Storing tomatoes after harvest

Ripe tomatoes should be stored at room temperature to retain great flavors. However, they stay fresh only for about two days. If you plan to store them for longer, immediately move your harvest to the refrigerator.

Unripe tomatoes should be stored in a cool and dark place and arranged in one layer. It is important to periodically check the harvest for cracks, holes and rot specks and immediately remove them. A single damaged tomato can cause rot in healthy tomatoes by transferring moisture.

David Oconner

Common Tomato Plant Diseases: Prevention, Care and Solutions

Like all fruit bearing crops, tomato plants are also susceptible to certain diseases and infections. The range of diseases that could potentially affect your tomato plantation depends on the plant variety, soil property, maintenance, the current season and the local climate. Diseases that commonly affect tomato plants are rarely fatal and can be controlled effectively if detected early.

Here are some common diseases that affect tomato plants and easy to follow solutions that ensure a great yield at the end of the season.

Wilts

Wilts are one of the most common diseases to affect tomato plants. However, most seedlings today are resistant to common wilt diseases. Wilts are generally caused by fungi infested soil.

Fusarium

The fusarium wilt first affects the lower leaves with initial symptoms of yellowing and subsequent drooping in a single stem. The symptoms start appearing on one side and eventually spread to the rest of the tomato plant. Fusarium attacks only tomato plants and can cause severe damage to the crop if left unchecked. Favored by warm temperatures and acidic pH of the soil, the fusarium fungus can survive in soil for years and can be transmitted through the seed.

Verticillium

Similar to fusarium, the verticillium fungus can survive in soil for upto eight years and cause more damage in alkaline soils. A tomato plant affected by verticillium starts out with yellowing of lower leaves and young shoots. The growth of the tomato plant is stunted as the leaf veins and shoots turn brown and eventually defoliate. Young shoots affected by verticillium eventually recover but most parts of the plant stop growing.

Countering wilts in tomato plants: Opting for disease resistant seedlings is the first step to prevent wilts from affecting your tomato plantation. Plant rotation and weeding are also important as they reduce the chance of the fungus growing in the soil. You should also ensure that all the old tomato plants and weeds affected by the disease are removed and destroyed. As wilts are internal infections, fungicides have no effect.

Rots

Rotting in different parts of tomato plants is a common occurrence in the rainy months and affects different varieties differently.

Timber rot

The white mold fungus is the main cause for timber rots that not only affects tomato plants, but also ornamental plants, beans and flowering plants. Coinciding with rainfall, this mold spreads rapidly during rains or if the soil is kept wet for prolonged durations. White mold affects the main stem as mushy brown infections spread around the tomato plant. If left unchecked, the rest of the plant eventually wilts and dies.

Soil rot

Soil rot mainly affect tomato fruits during rainy seasons. If the fruits are touching the ground, they could develop small brown rots that eventually lead to the fruits cracking open.

Solutions for tomato plant rots: There are no solutions to cure timber rot. As a gardener, you can only ensure to plant tomatoes away from vulnerable plant varieties of beans and ornamental flowers. Avoid excess overhead irrigation to keep the plant from developing rots. Staking tomato plants keep the fruits from touching the ground and help reduce soil rot to a great extent.

Fungal diseases

Tomato plants are most commonly affected by fungal diseases. Mostly air borne, these diseases spread quicker in cool and wet weathers. Dew and rain also contribute to spreading fungal infections that often lead to spots and blights on tomato plants, eventually leading to yellowing and leaf drop.

Septoria blight

The Septoria leaf spot usually appears after the first fruits are borne and affects lower leaves. The spots are generally small and circular with gray centers dotted with tiny black spots and outlined by dark margins. Rarely affecting fruits, Septoria blight sometimes affects vines and upper leaves.

Early blight

Early blight appears after a full fruit set and attacks the lower leaves first. Forming large, dark and roughly circular spots on the leaves, early blight eventually affects the upper leaves at temperatures ranging from 75° F to 85° F. These spots then develop concentric rings which lead to yellowing and severe defoliation. The early blight sometimes damages stems and fruits and cause dropping before full maturity.

Late blight

Similar to other fungal diseases, late blight occurs in moist and cool climates. Late blight affects the edges of leaves, forming dark green spots without a definite shape or margin. If the local temperature stays above 86° F, you will not have to worry about late blight. The spots appear wet and greasy and sometimes affect fruits.

Solutions for fungal diseases: An easy way to prevent fungal infections from affecting the leaves of tomato plants is to rotate crops. As fall approaches, ensure that you remove and break down tomato vines to avoid further infection. If you have detected fungal growth in the early stages, remove the affected parts of the plant to prevent further damage. Avoid using sprinklers and water the plants at the base. Regularly use fungicides to prevent any chances of spreading.

Bacterial diseases

Bacterial diseases affecting tomato plants are mainly due to infected seedlings. Specks and spots formed on leaves, fruits and stems of tomato plants spread rapidly in warm and humid areas.

Bacterial leaf specks

The bacterium that causes specks in tomato plants is mainly transmitted through seeds and grows rapidly between the temperatures of 55° F to 77° F. These bacterial specks can occur on leaves and fruits and leave small brown circular specks that are slightly raised.

Bacterial spot

This seed borne bacterium spreads through infected transplants and affects the leaves and immature fruits on tomato plants. Producing scabby circular spots on the surface, these bacteria can also spread through infected weeds. Rain, dew, humidity and warm temperatures favor the growth of these bacteria.

Bacterial canker

Bacterial canker is a comparatively uncommon disease but can severely affect your crop yield if left unattended. Mainly caused by diseased seeds, these bacteria sometimes dwell in soil, dead stems, and older tomato plants. Although they are seed borne, these bacteria spread quickly if humid and wet weather conditions persist.

Tomato plants infected by bacterial canker often wilt, starting with lower leaves. Affecting the outer edges of leaves with raised white spots and blisters, this disease can affect all parts of the plant.

Solutions for bacterial diseases: Bacterial spots and specks can be managed by using disease-free seeds and transplants, and growing them in sterilized pots. Crop rotation also helps reduce the chances of spreading this bacterium. It is also important to get rid of weeds and old tomato plants before planting a new set. If you detect bacterial infections on your tomato plant, immediately spray copper based fungicides to control the disease.

Viral diseases

Distortion and mottling of tomato plant leaves and fruits are most commonly caused by viral diseases. These diseases can spread through different methods and can be controlled to a certain extent with a few precautions.

Spotted wilt

Although spotted wilt cannot be easily detected, one of the most common initial symptoms of this viral infection is the presence of orange spots or bronzed shading of young leaves. While older leaves usually become brownish before dying, younger shoots develop dark streaks and eventually lead to the death of the plant. Infections caused in young plants can lead to death while in older plants, developing tomato fruits are affected.

Controlling spotted wilt: As spotted wilt in tomato plants are mainly transmitted through larval thirps, there are few methods to control this infection. Separate vegetable hosts from flowers and control weeds to reduce the chances of spreading the virus. While purchasing the plants for your garden, ensure that they appear extremely robust and healthy.

Tobacco mosaic

Tobacco mosaic virus causes tomato leaves to become mottled with light and dark green spots. The plant growth is stunted and the leaves become rough and fern-like. Tobacco mosaic virus does not affect tomato fruits as severely but may cause uneven ripening and size reduction.

In serious cases, the virus may affect the fruit as they develop brown streaks and green spots. This virus is mainly seed borne and can sometimes be transmitted manually through plants, clothing, gardening tools and the gardeners themselves.

Cucumber mosaic

Mainly spread through aphids, cucumber mosaic may also spread mechanically. The early symptoms of infection include yellowing of leaves and stunted plants. The plants may sometimes develop a bushy appearance and the leaves become elongated and distorted.

Preventing mosaic virus: Since the virus actually spreads from debris in tobacco products, avoid handling tobacco plants and products while cultivating tomato plants. Ensure that you wash your tools and hands thoroughly to prevent the virus from spreading. Detergent is known to inactivate this virus and works better than regular soap. Avoid planting susceptible plant varieties near tomato plants to reduce chances of viral infection.

Non-parasitic diseases

Apart from parasites and other micro-organisms, tomato plants can also be affected by physiological abnormalities. Non-parasitic disorders are very common and can be controlled with a few precautionary measures.

Sunscald

When fruits are suddenly exposed to sunlight, they may develop light spots that develop into blisters. If left unchecked, these blisters turn whitish and become sunken. Severe sunscald may result in sudden dropping of leaves, similar to the effects of leaf spot infections.

Preventing sunscald: The ill-effects of sunscald can be easily controlled by using caution against leaf infections and providing adequate shade from harsh sunlight.

Blossom end rot

First appearing as a light water logged spot on immature fruits, blossom end rot eventually turns black and leathery. Calcium deficiency, fluctuations in soil moisture, and excessive amounts of nitrogen or ammonium fertilizers and root pruning can cause blossom end rot.

Preventing blossom end rot: One of the most important steps you should take to protect your tomato plantation from blossom end root is to protect the roots. Avoid planting seeds too close to each other. Use fertilizers that are rich in phosphorous and nitrate. Avoid sudden change in water supply and ensure that the tomato plants are uniformly watered at regular intervals.

Use a mulch (organic or plastic) to ensure uniform supply of moisture and avoid supplying too much or too little water. Clear plastic mulches are known to work best with tomato plants as they warm the soil effectively while creating a stronger root system.

Growth cracks

Cracks on stems and fruits occur during the high growth periods of warm and rainy weather. The severity of the cracks depends on the contrast in weather i.e. the growth cracks are more severe if the rainy weather follows an extremely dry period. These cracks may develop concentrically around the stem end of the fruit. Different varieties of tomato plants have varying susceptibilities to growth cracks.

Catface

Catface commonly develops on blossom ends of tomato fruits and is most commonly a result of cold weather. Deep cavities, puckering and swollen protuberances are the most common catface abnormalities detected in tomatoes. The vulnerability towards catface changes with different varieties of tomato plants.

Leaf roll

Reported mainly during rainy seasons, leaf roll causes tomato leaves to roll up and become leathery and thick. Cold and humid weather, excessive fertilizing or pruning can result in leaf roll. However, precautionary measures are not required as this phenomenon has no grave effect on the growth of the plant or the crop yield.

Herbicide injury

Tomato plants are generally sensitive to growth regulating herbicides and the leaves may develop a cupped look, causing them to become leathery and thick. In severe cases, the growth of the tomato plant may be stunted or abnormal.

Preventing herbicide injury: To combat injuries caused by herbicides, avoid using solutions containing 2, 4-D on tomato plants as they thicken leaves. If you are using this herbicide on other plants in your lawn, beware that the fumes emitted from the herbicide may affect tomato plants. Ensure that you spray this solution from a considerable distance to avoid affecting your tomato plantation.

Conclusion

Tomatoes are wonderful additions to any home garden. They can be incorporated in a variety of dishes, and offer multiple health benefits. A garden with bright red tomato plants is a joy to behold. Armed with the right knowledge, you can have the tomato garden of your dreams. Of course, care and affection, from the time of planting until harvesting and through the plant's lifecycle, also plays a role in ensuring sustained and healthy produce.

About The Author

David Oconner has been writing and publishing books on many of his varied interests. He has books on topics such as Cichlid Fish, How to Grow Tomatoes, Sugar Gliders, How to Play Minecraft and more.

Printed in Great Britain
by Amazon

34230358R00031